Diana NaNa Ferrer

Nature Vibes

An Adult Coloring Book

- @artbynana305
- @artbynana305
- Facebook.com/Dianananaferrer

Copyright © 2017 by Diana NaNa Ferrer
Thank you for your support and for complying with copyright laws by not reproducing, scanning, or distributing any part of this book without written permission from the author.

This book is dedicated to my daughter, Layla, who at 18 months old already loves to color. I would also like to dedicate this book to my loving husband, Roberto, who has been very supportive of my creative endeavors, my sisters Joanna, Talia, and Sofia whom inspired 3 characters in this book, and to my parents and step parents, who have all been very supportive and encouraging.

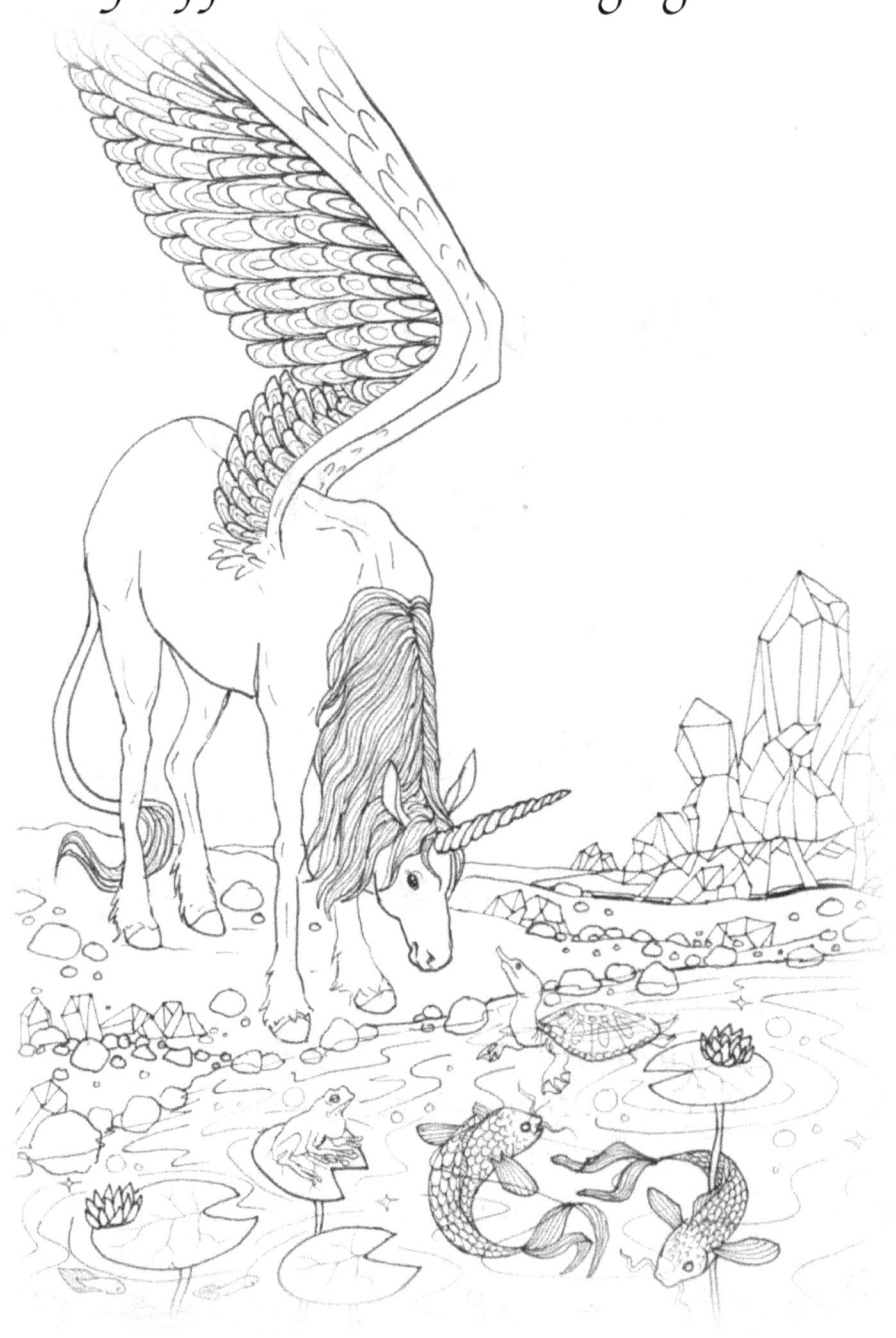

Use this page to test out your art materials.

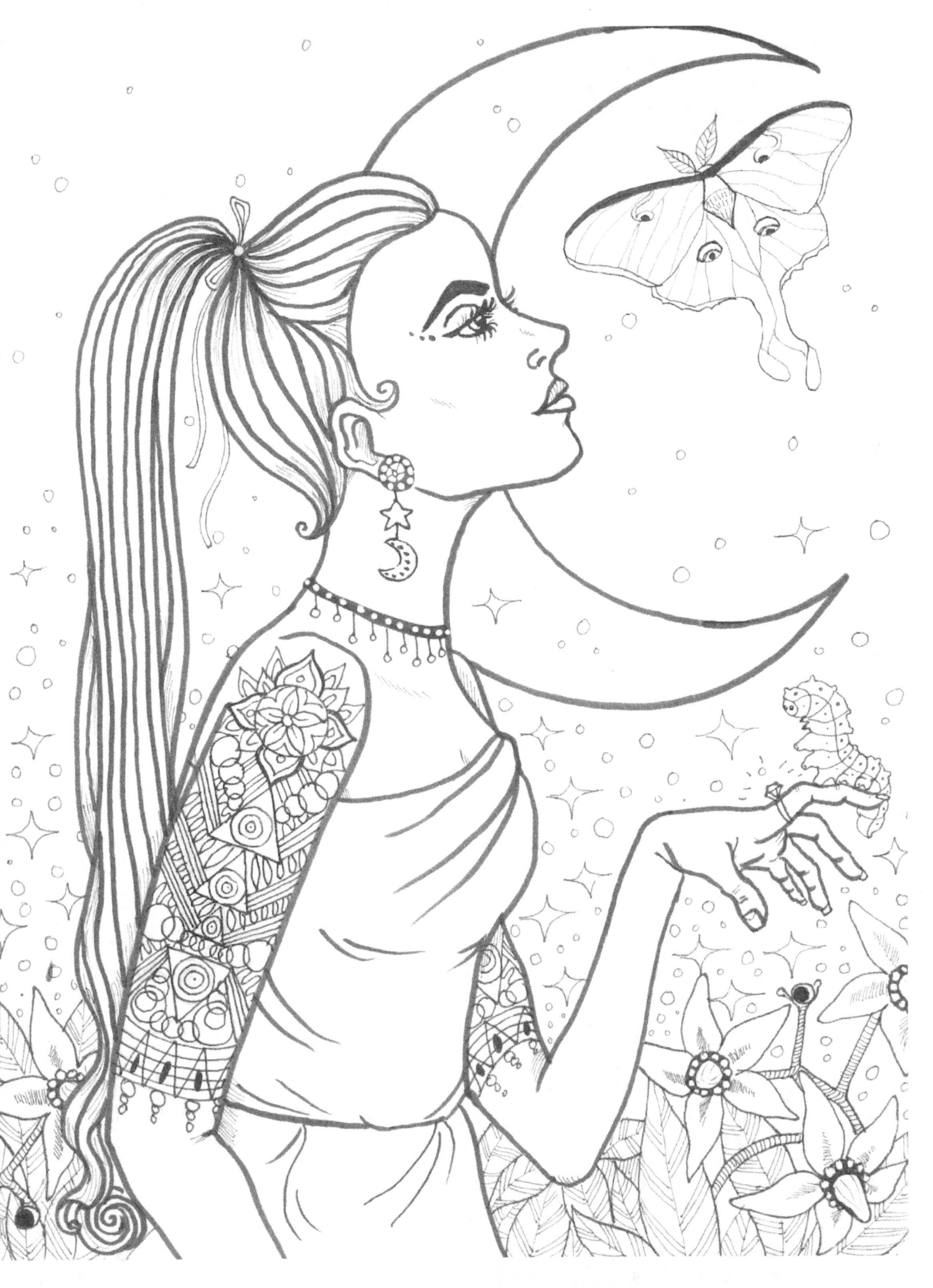

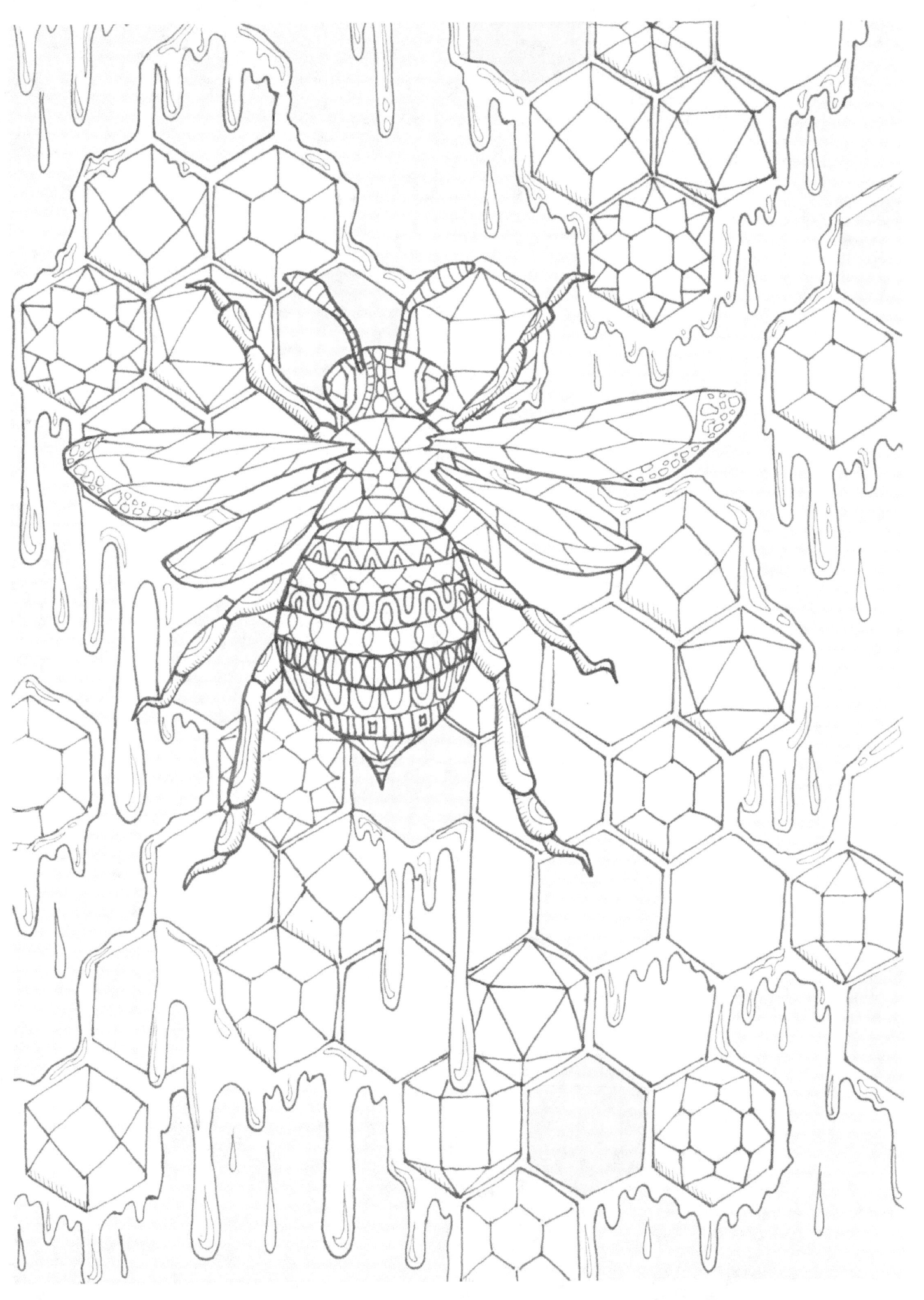

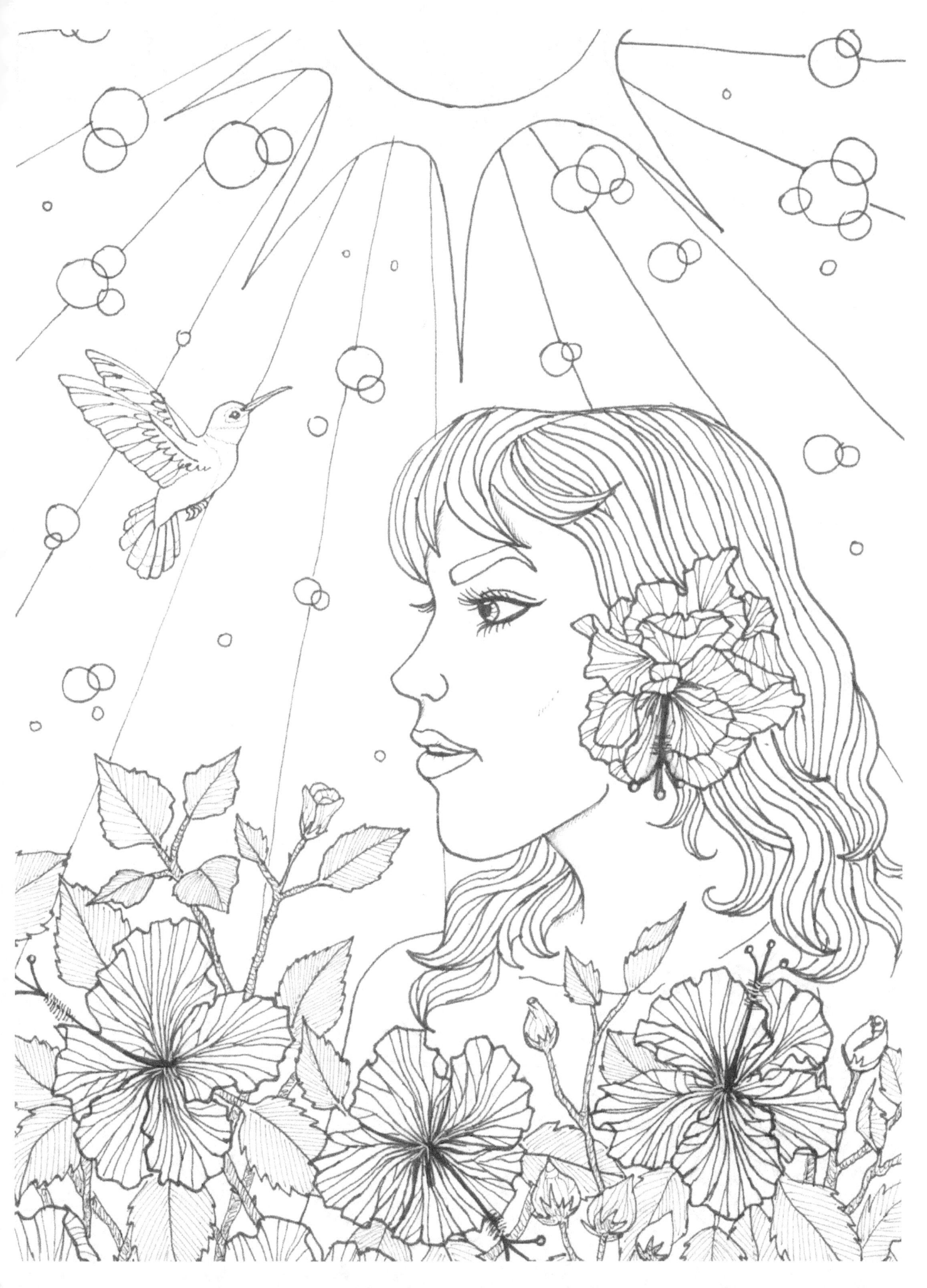

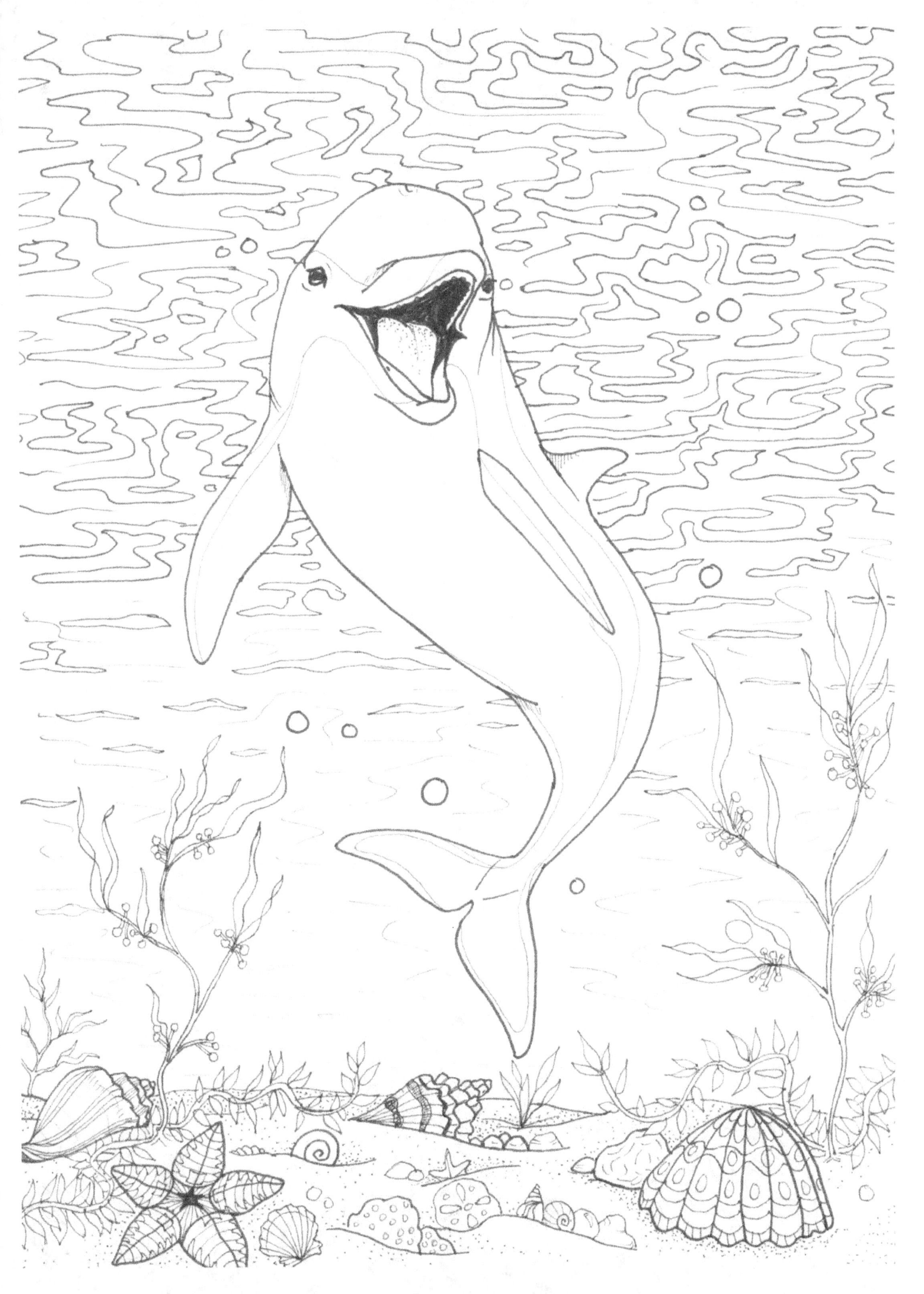

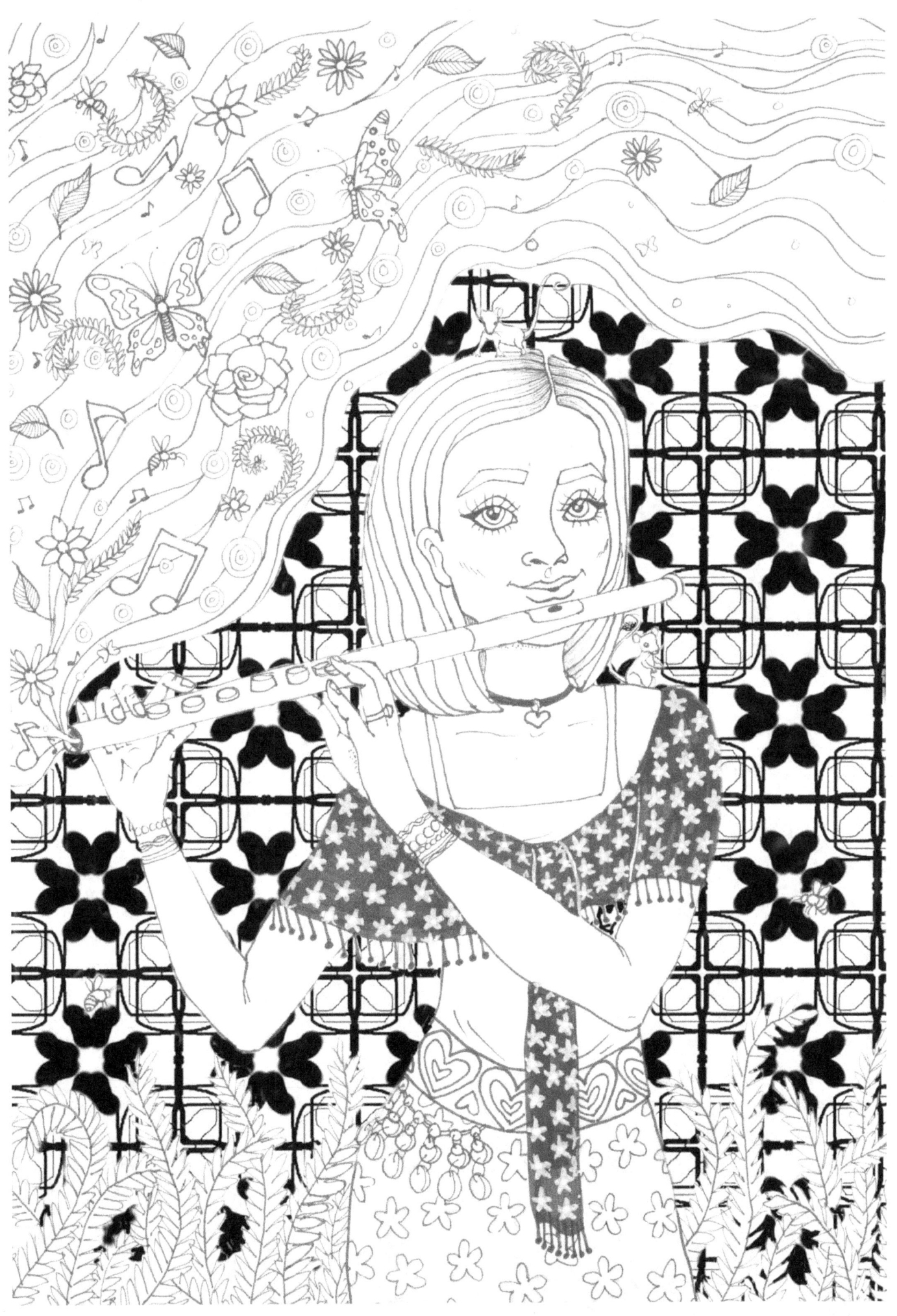

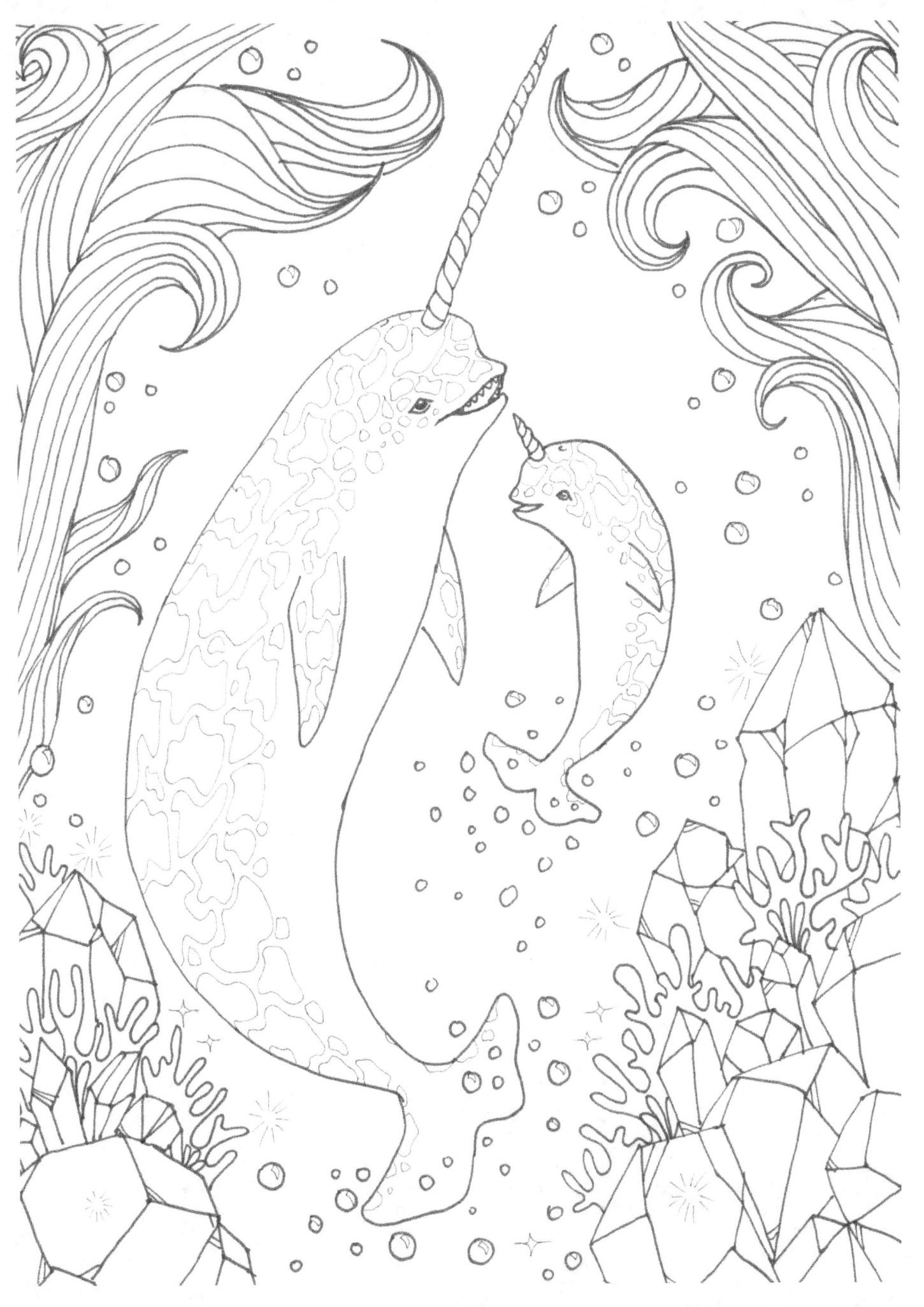

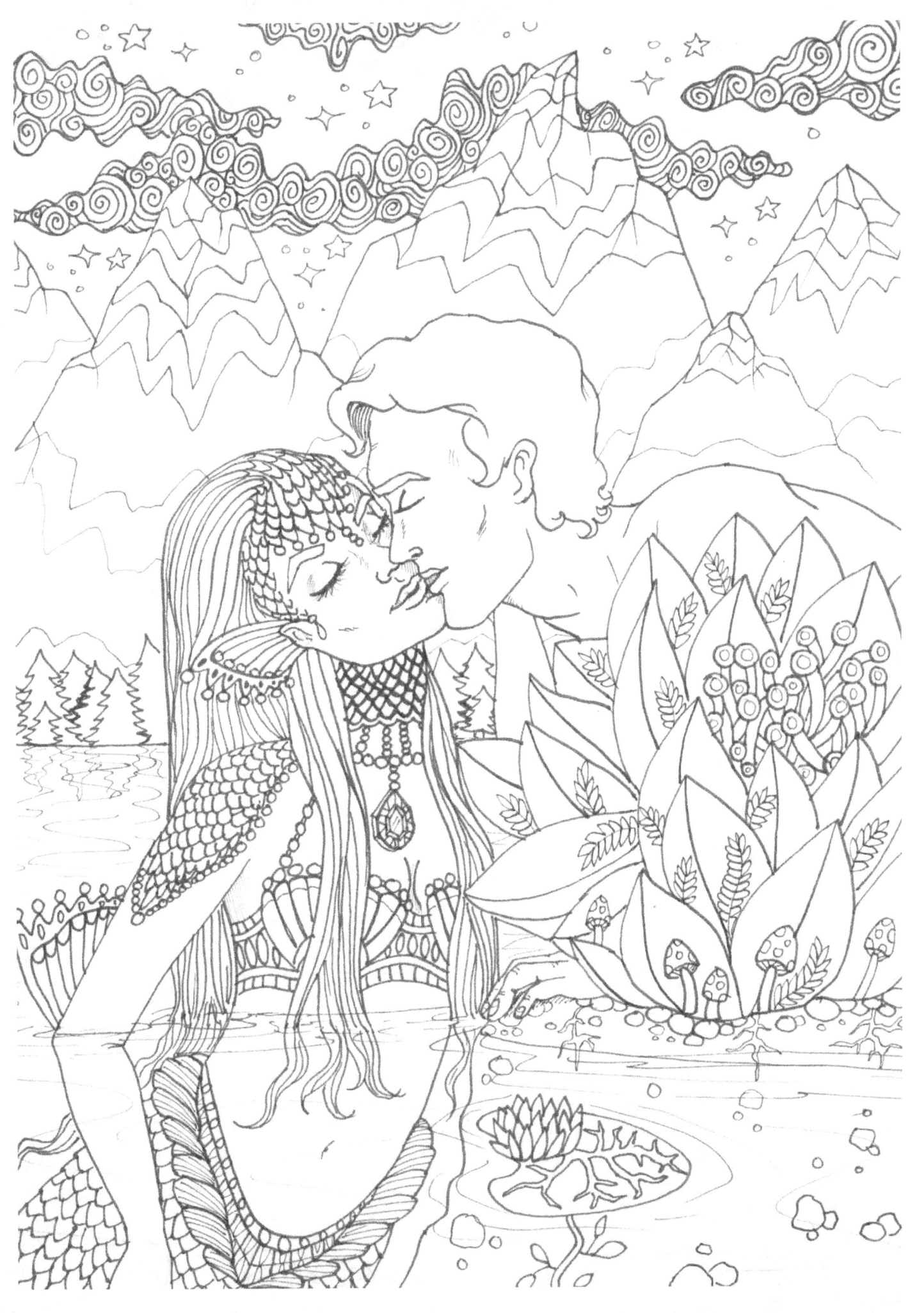

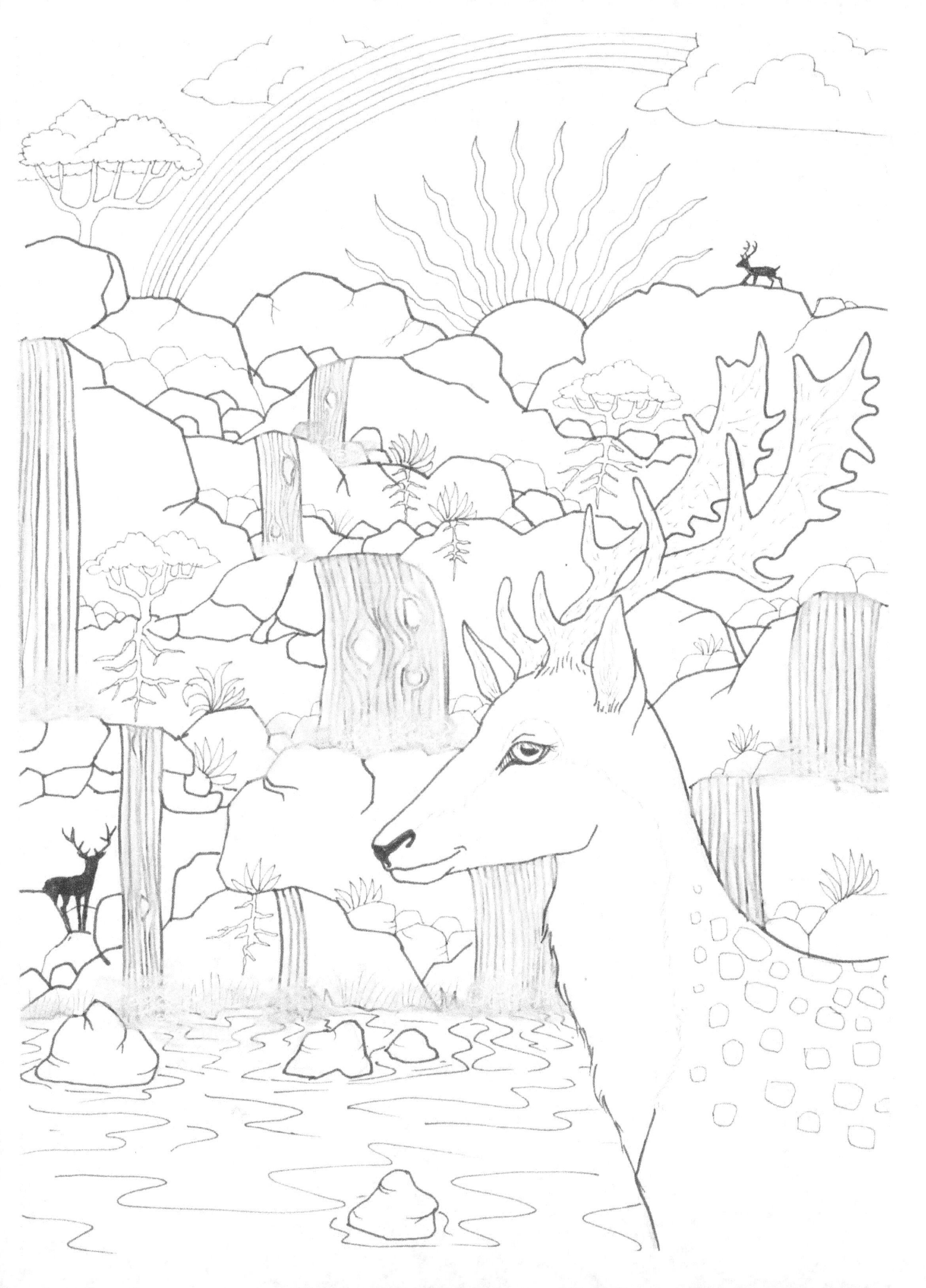

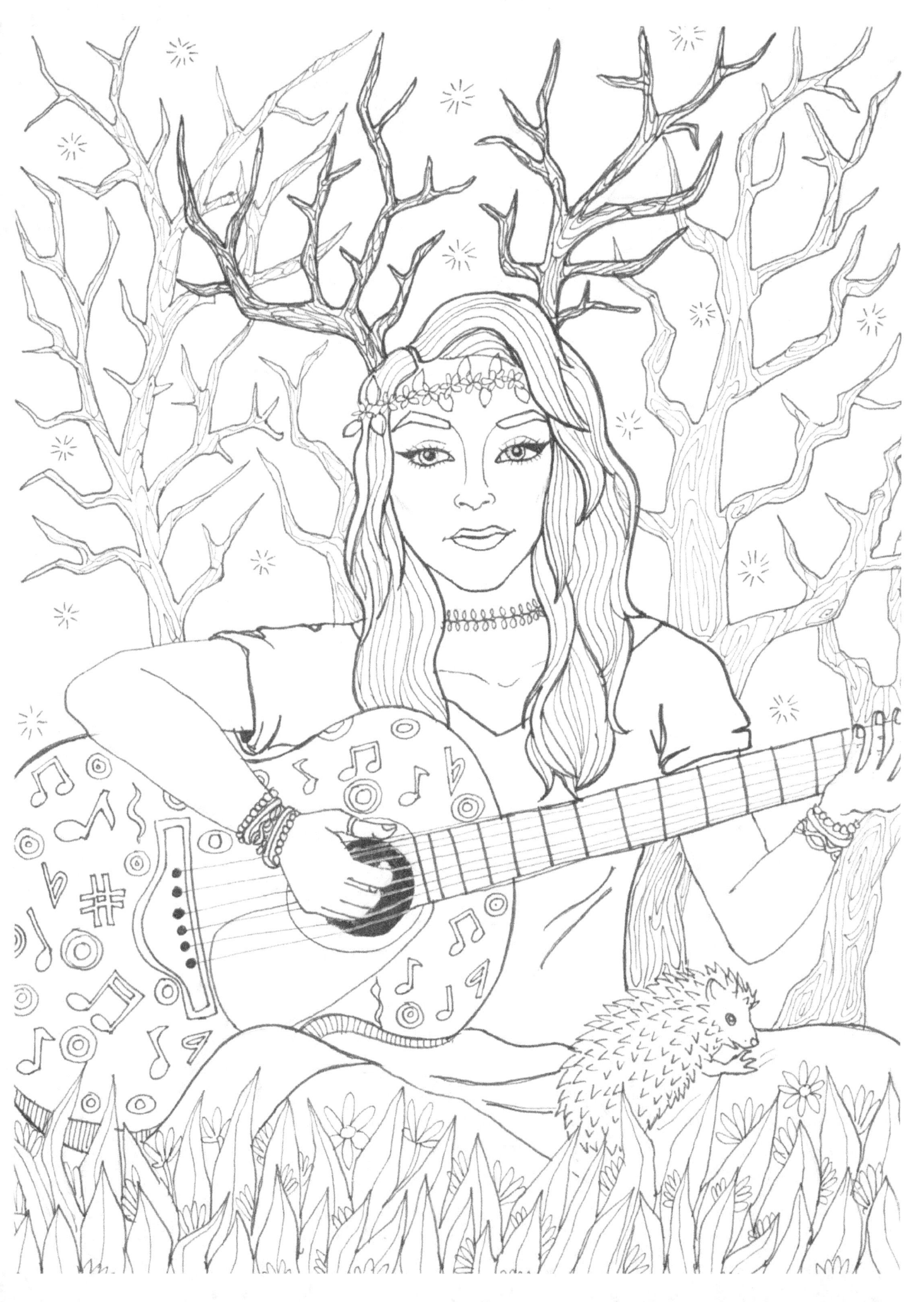

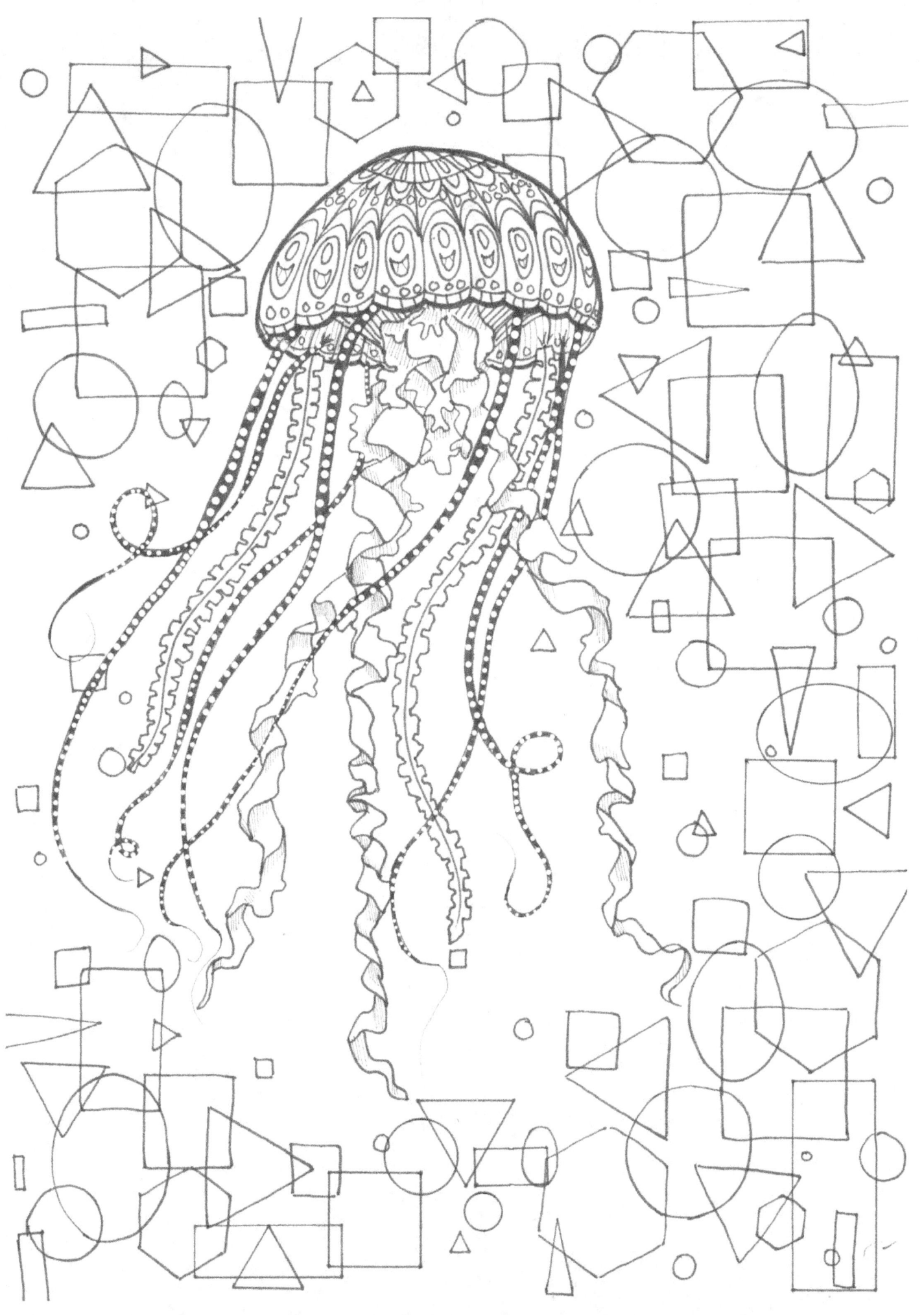

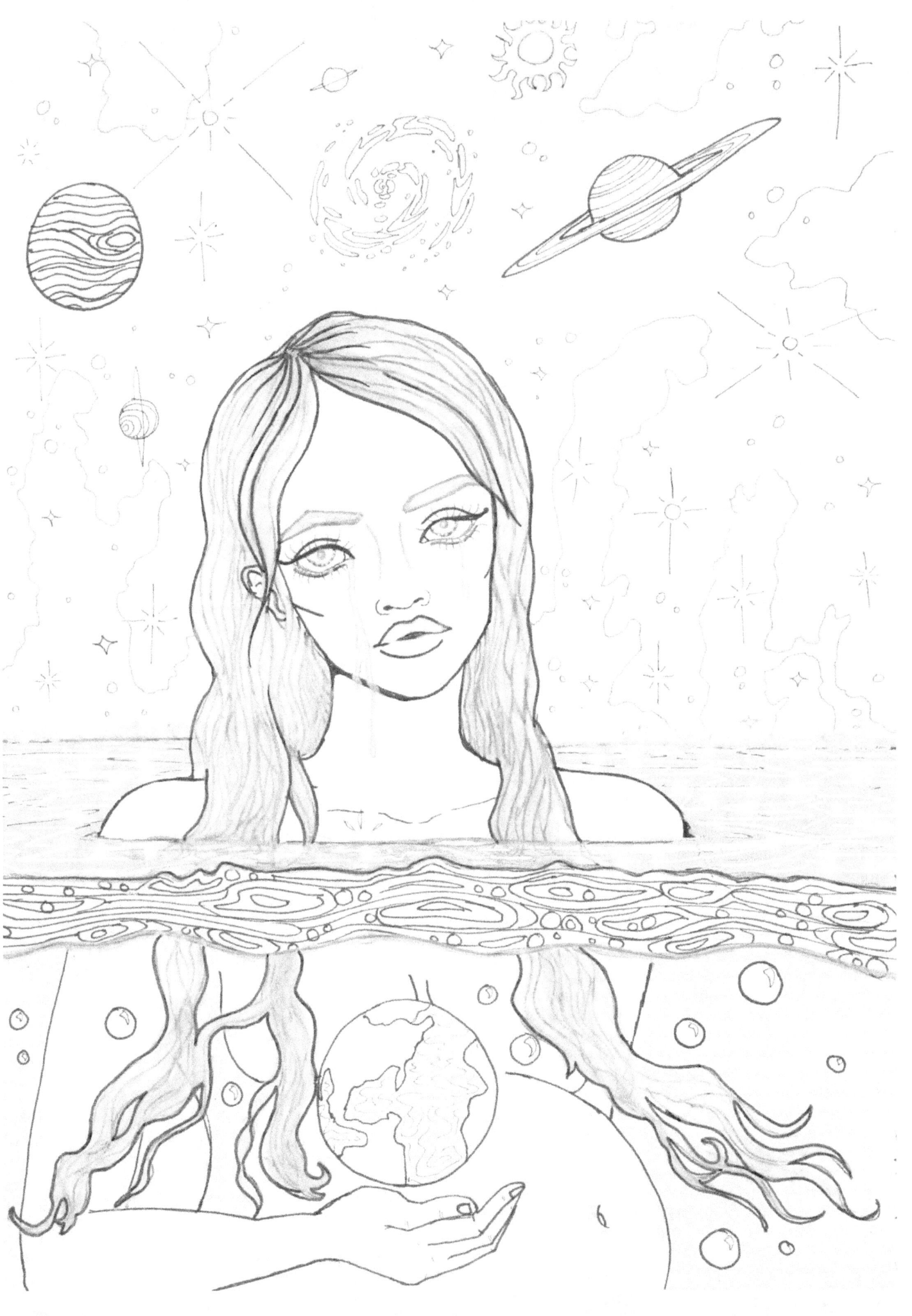

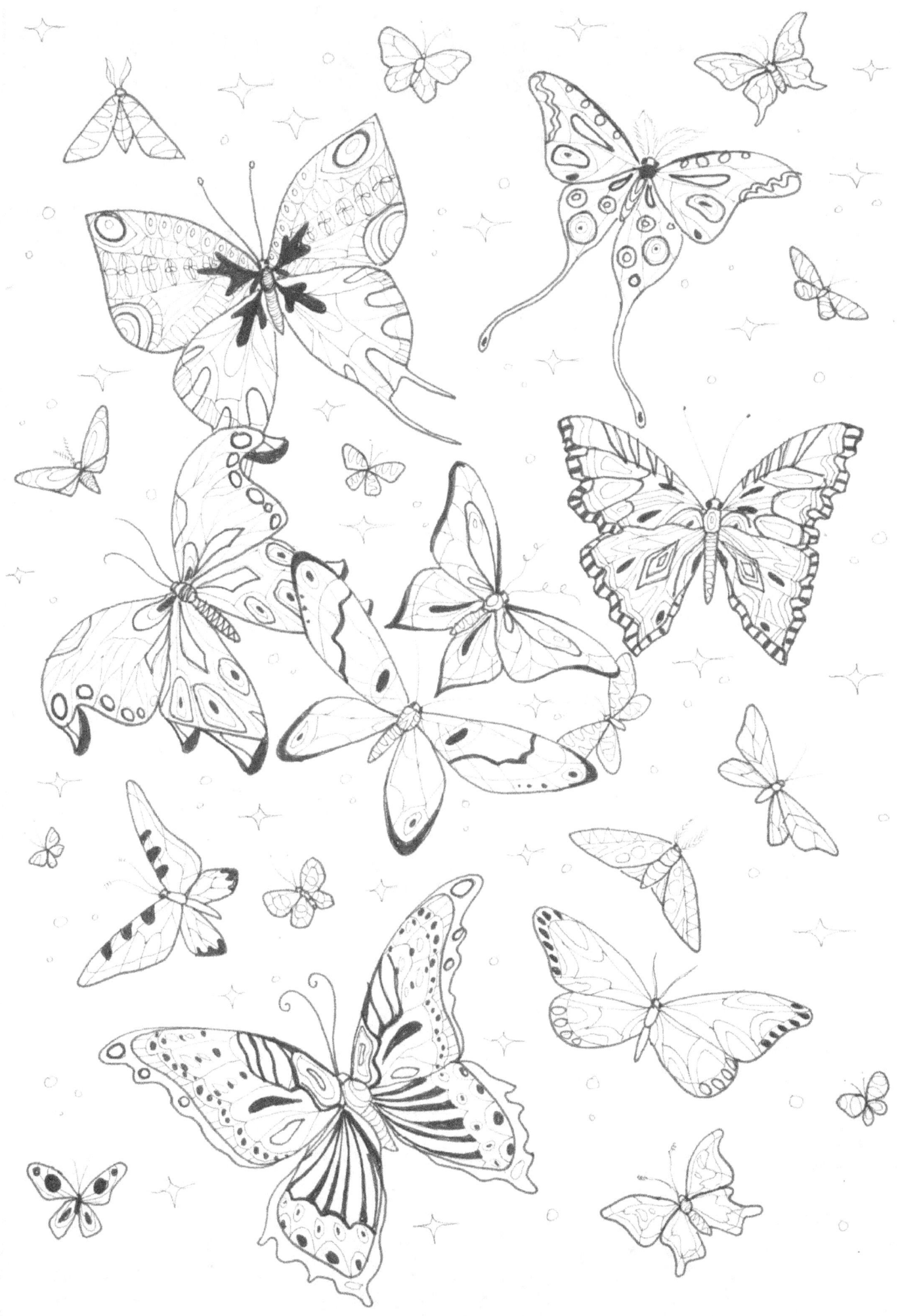

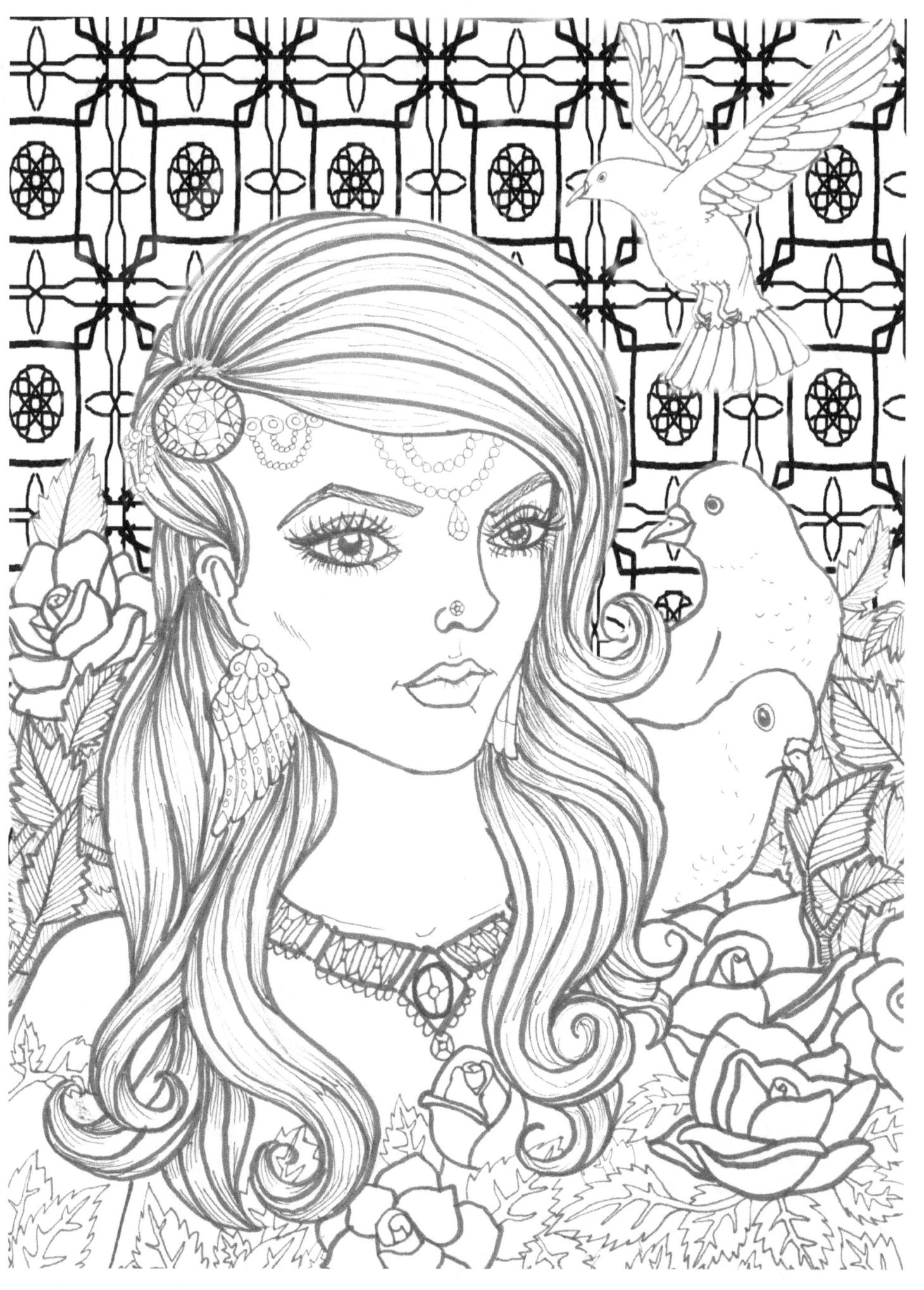

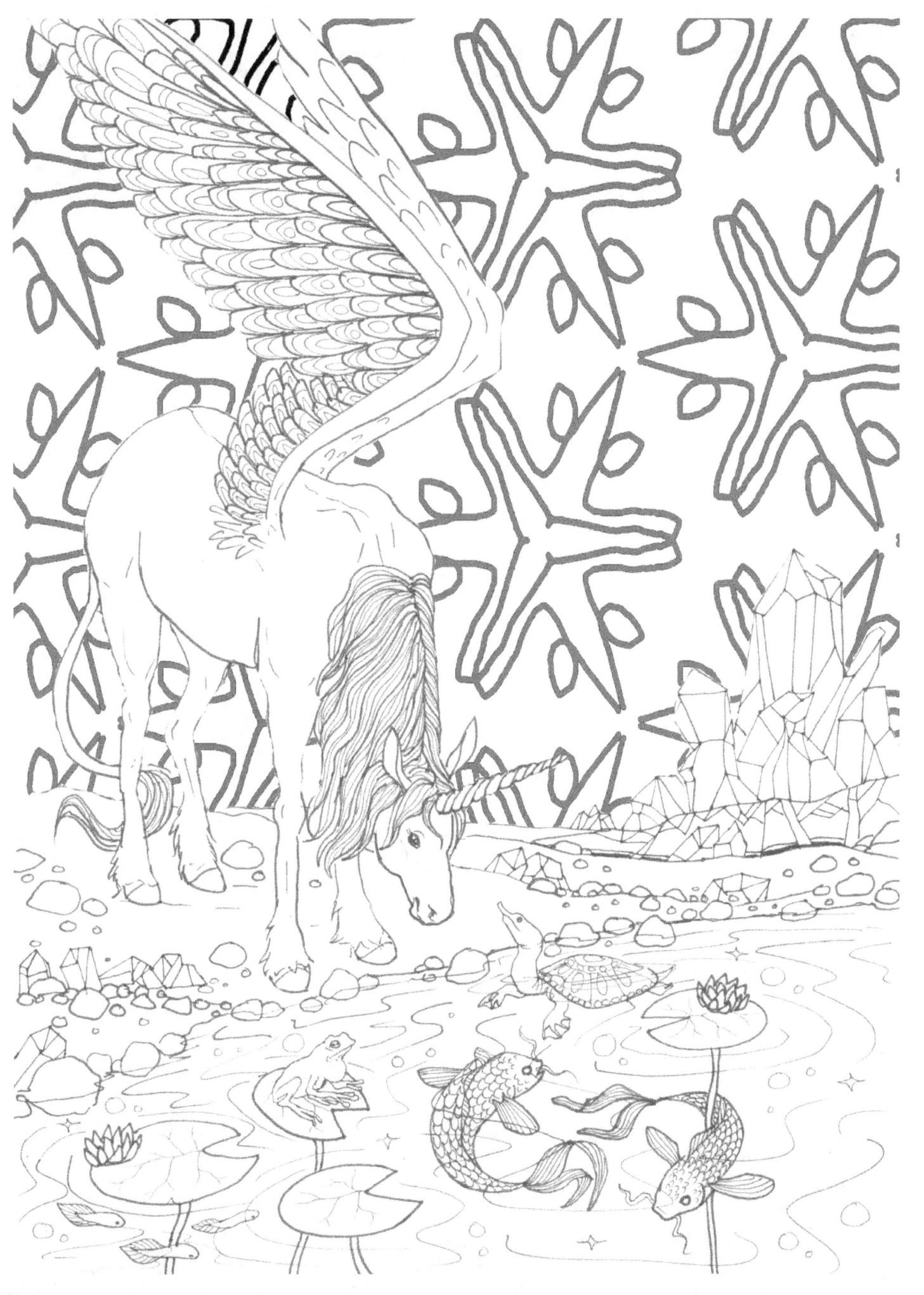

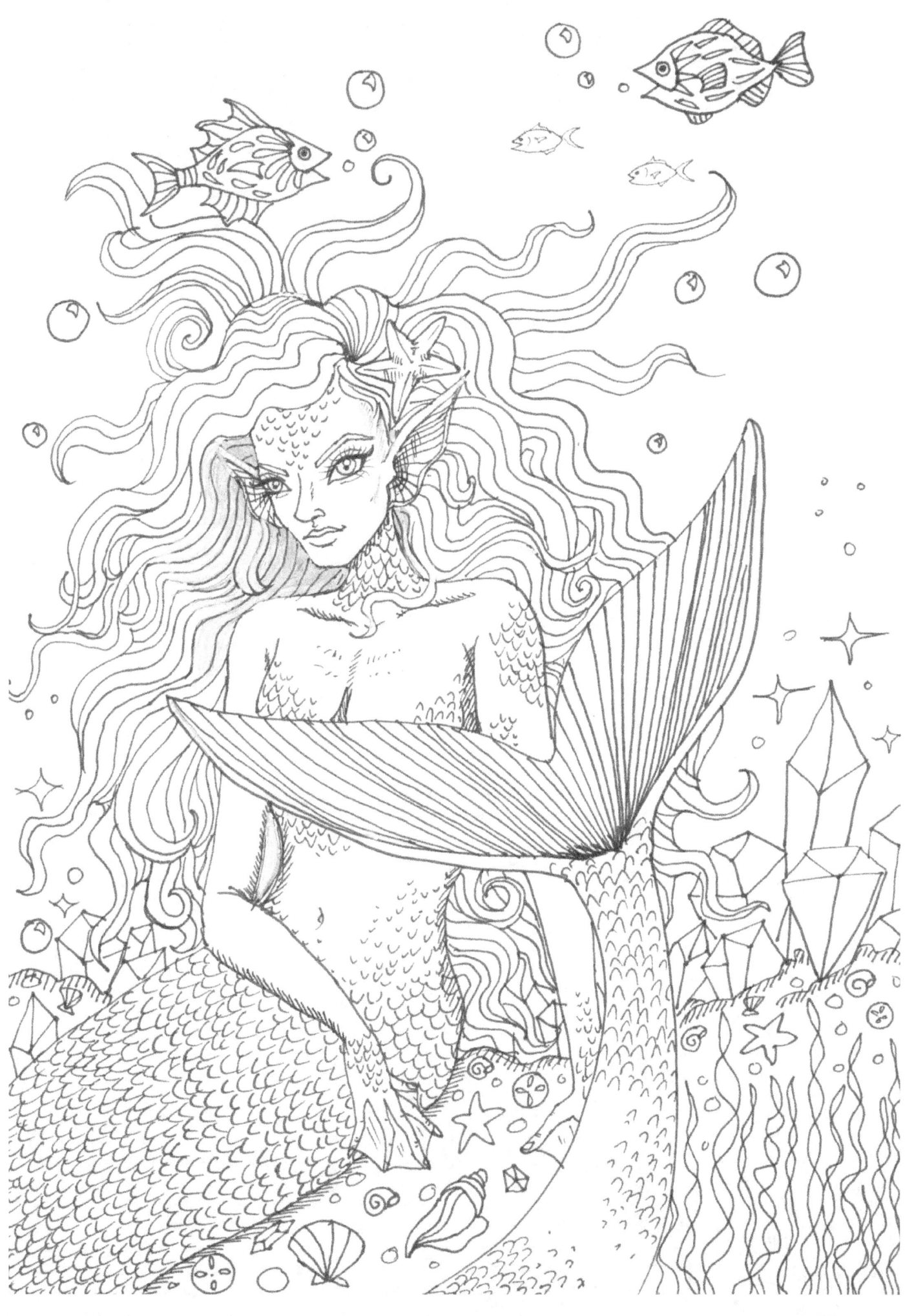

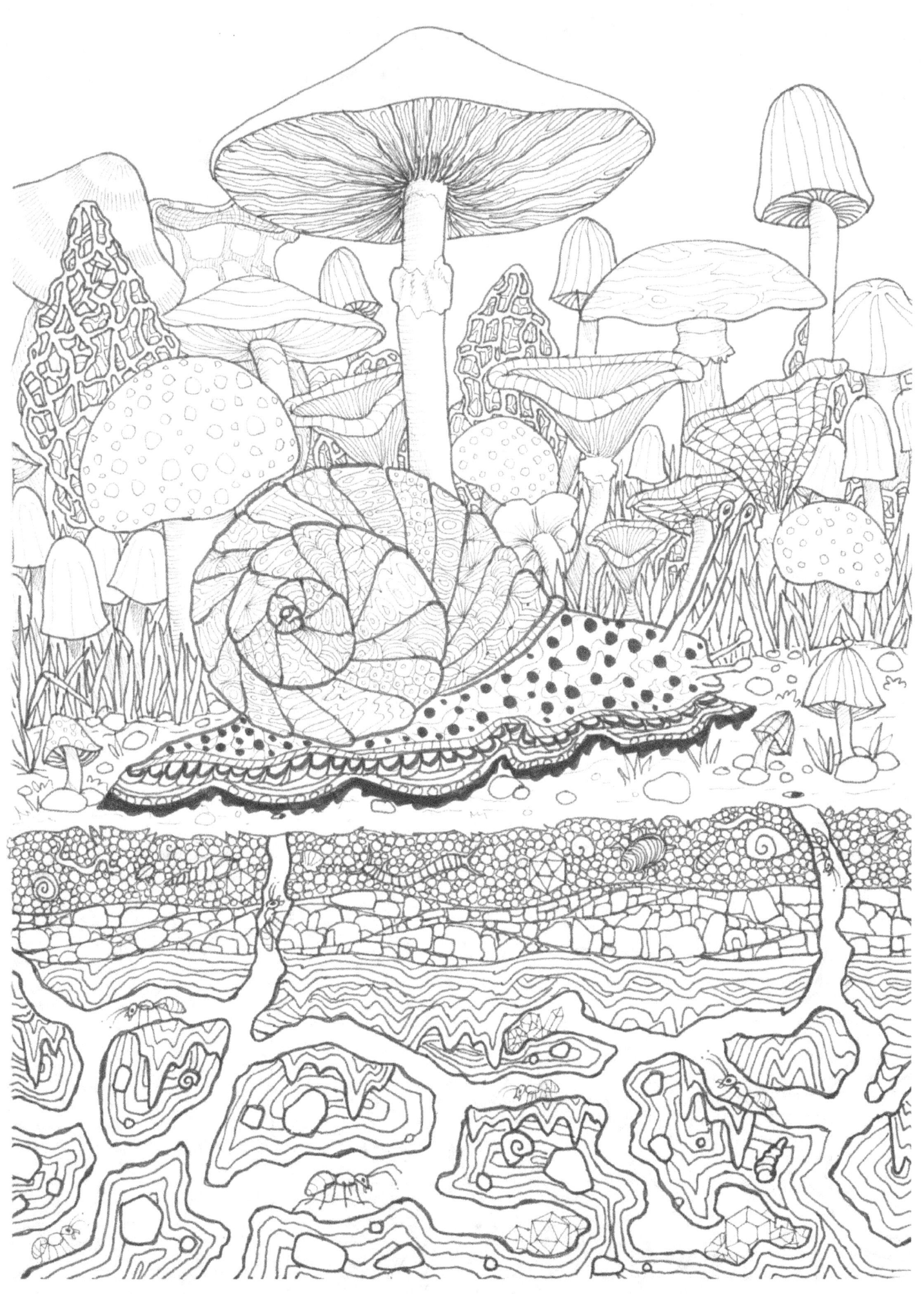

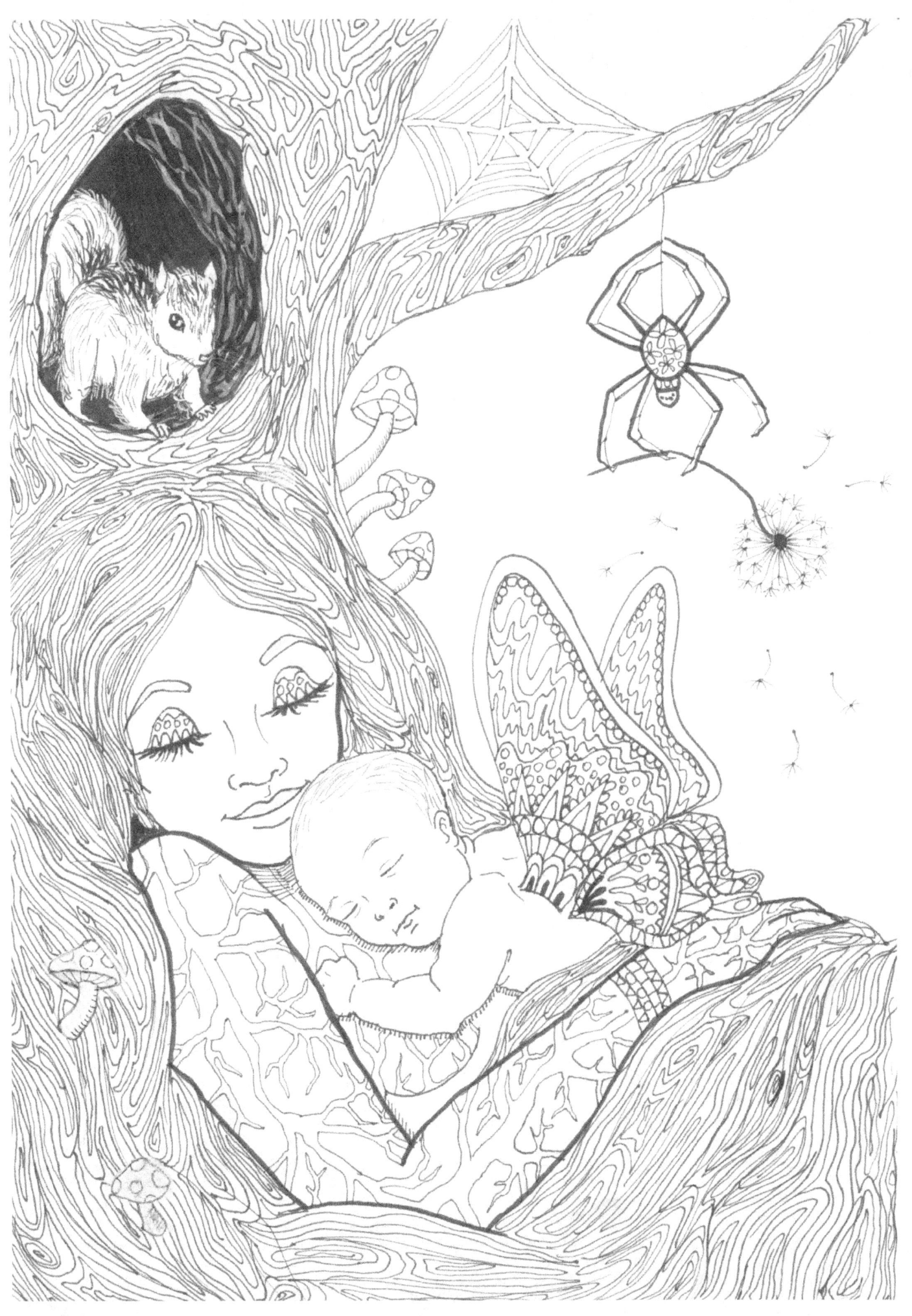

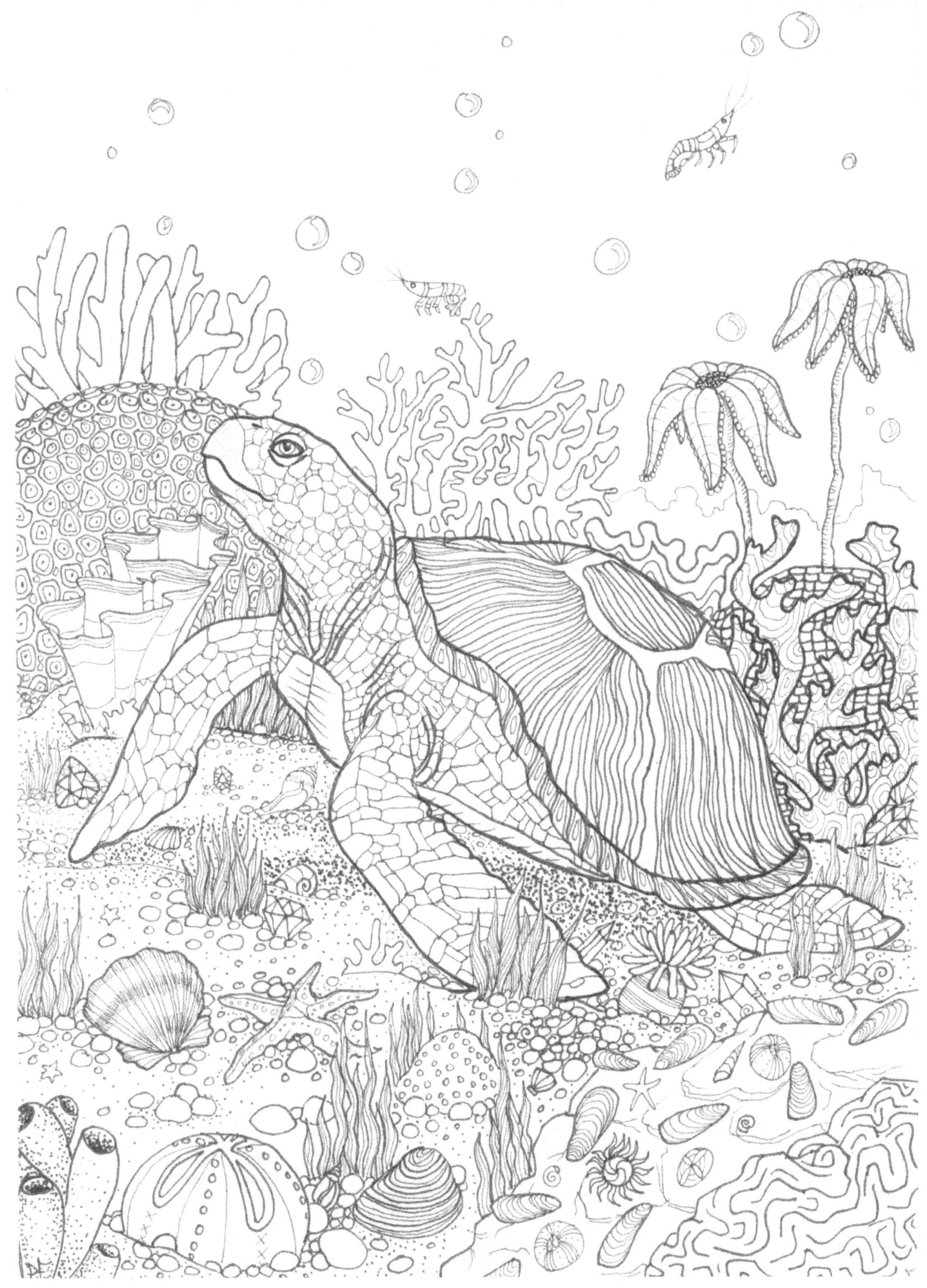

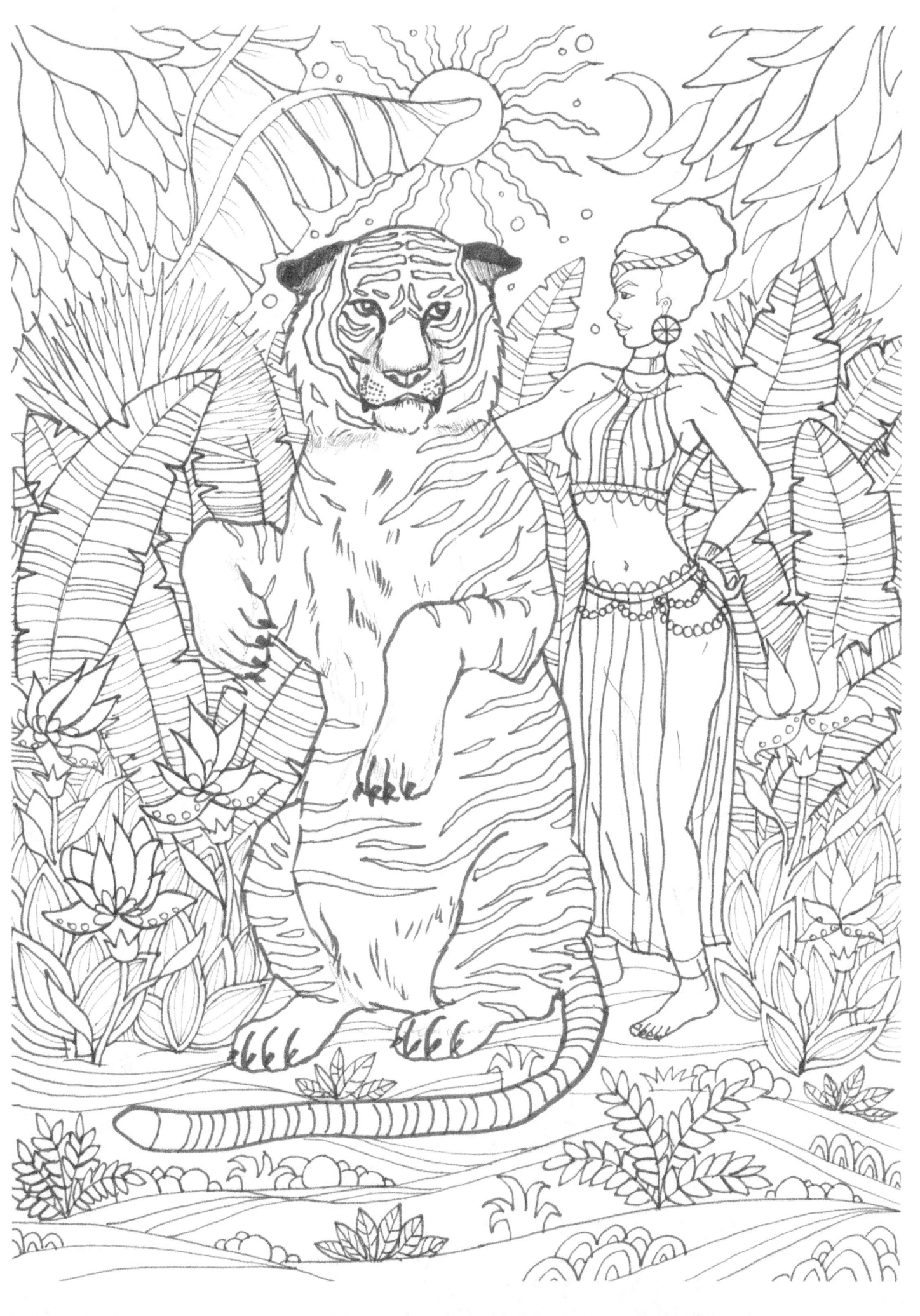

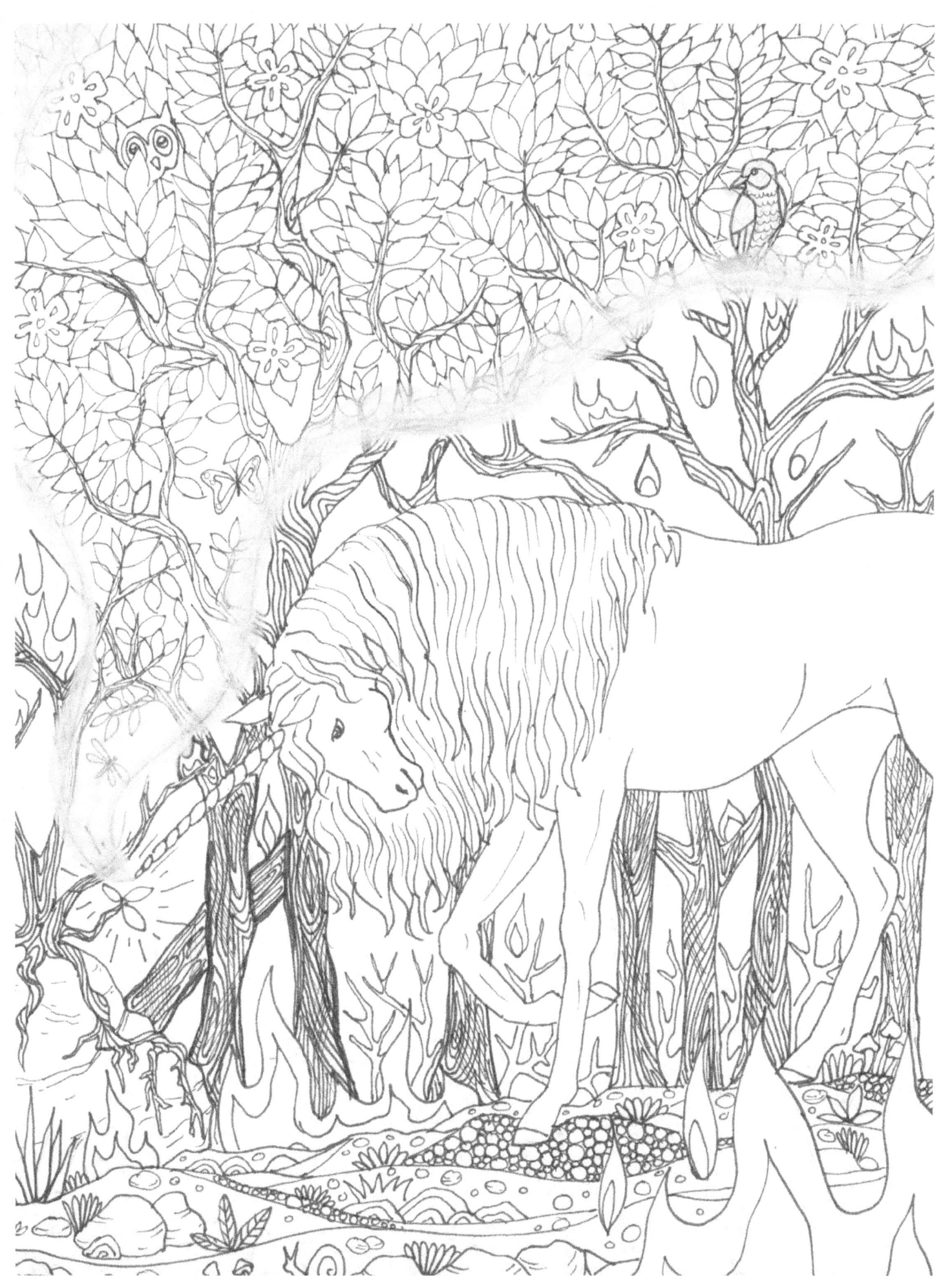

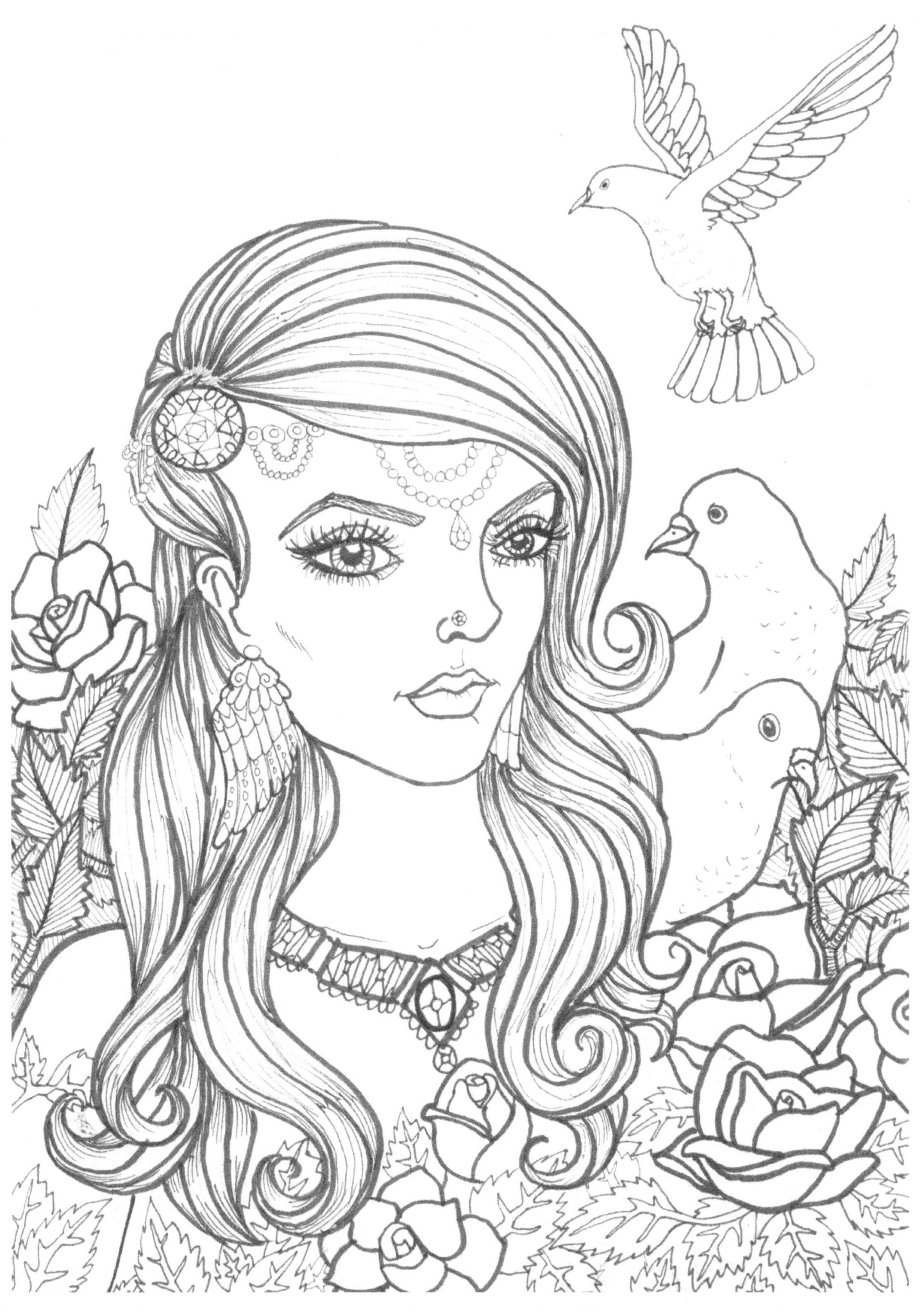

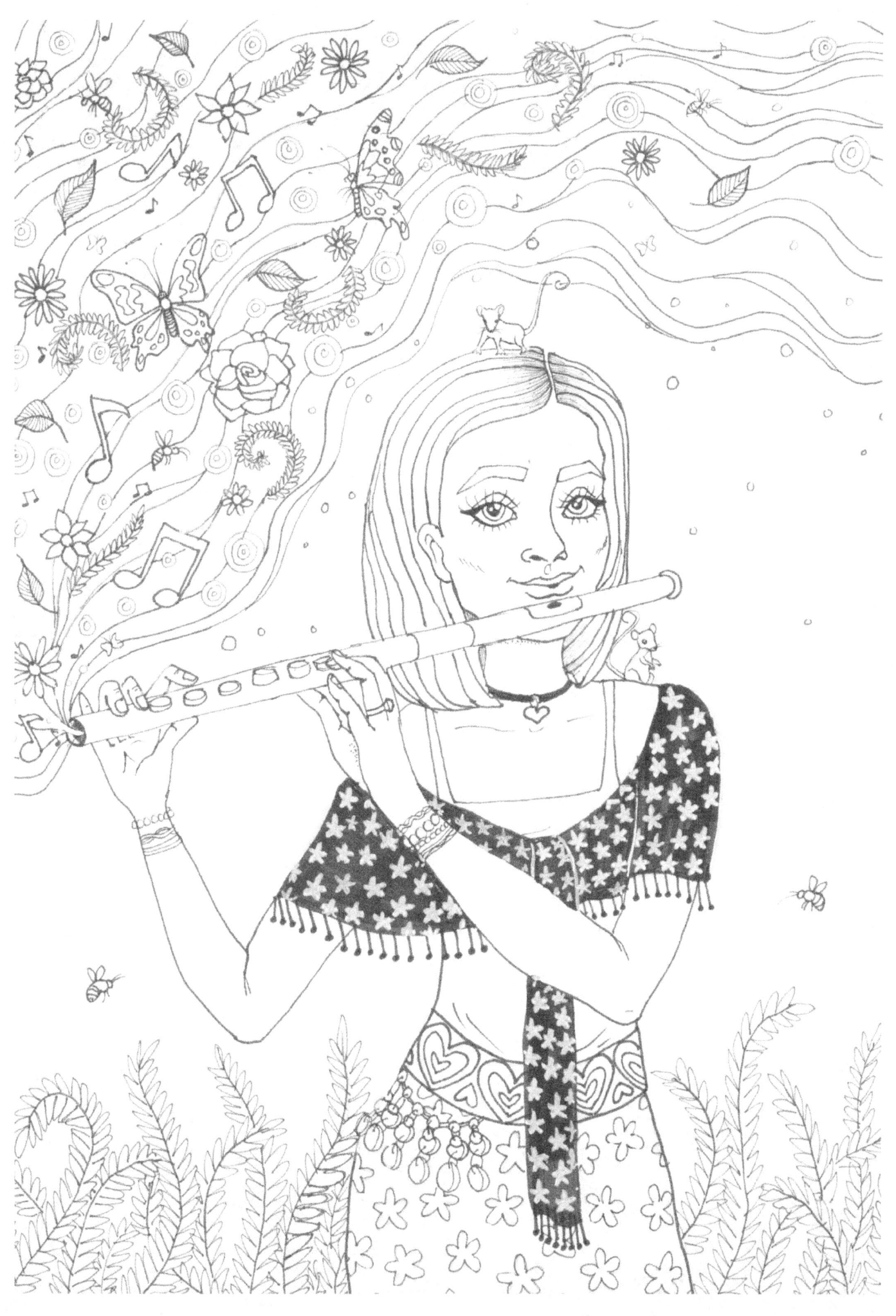

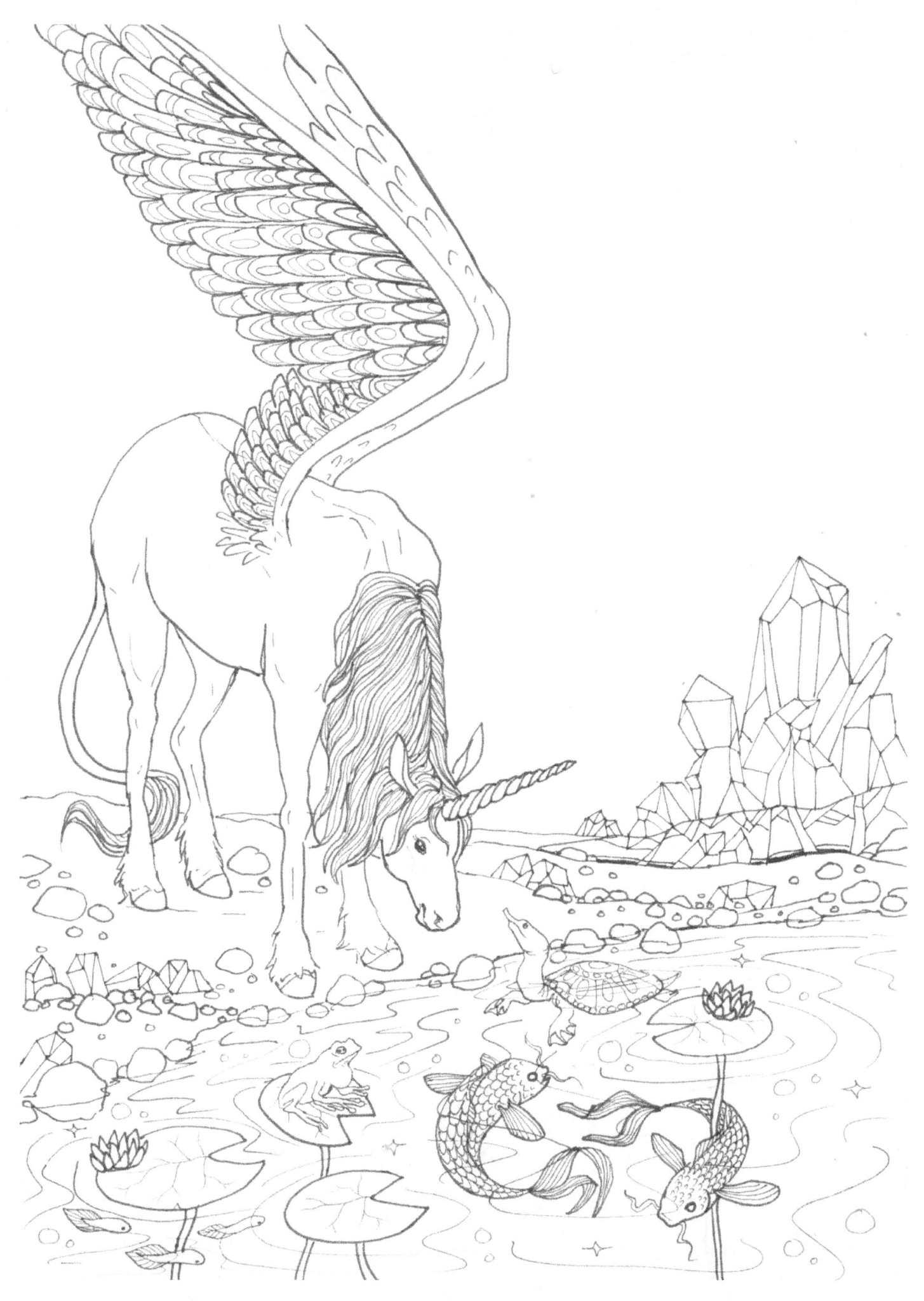

www.ingramcontent.com/pod-product-compliance
Lightning Source LLC
Chambersburg PA
CBHW081307180526
45170CB00007B/2600